THROWING STICKS AT RECESS

Poems from the Schoolyard

THROWING STICKS AT RECESS

Poems from the Schoolyard

by
Ivan Kershner

Clare Songbirds
Publishing House

Clare Songbirds Publishing House Poetry Series
ISBN 978-1-957221-16-8
Clare Songbirds Publishing House
Throwing Sticks at Recess© 2024 Ivan Kershner

Cover art © 2024 Lynn Kershner

Printed in the United States of America
FIRST EDITION

140 Cottage Street
Auburn, New York 13021
www.claresongbirdspub.com

As a public school educator, principal, assistant superintendent, college professor, and occasional inept boiler fixer and snow shoveler, I have spent over forty-two years in the classrooms and corridors of schools in four states. I have worked with thousands of children from kindergarten through college, and hundreds of inspiring and creative teachers. Rest assured that each of these poems had its seed first planted following a true interaction with a child.

~Ivan "Mr. Ivan" Kershner

Table of Contents

Recess Ain't Easy 1
Recipe for Trouble 2
Remembering 3
All the Stuff I Know 4
Assigned Reading 5
Braces 6
Bringing Elephants to School 7
"Bus Left!" 8
Cafeteria 9
Capturing Kids' Hearts 10
Caught in a Daydream 11
Cheerleaders 12
Crayons 13
"Don't Call on Me!" List 14
Dressing in Style 15
Excuse ME! 16
Figurative Language...NOT! 17
Final Score: 35-0 18
Friday 20
Geography 21
Gravity 22
Guarantees for Kids 23
Hall Lockers 24
Halloween Dinner 25
Halloween 26
Homework 27
"I almost remember..." 28
If Sixth Grade Ran the World 29
Inside Recess 30
Lipstick 31
Locker Clean-Out 32
Lost 'n Found 33
Math Grade 34
Retention 35
The South Carolina Sleigh Ride 36
School Bus 37
Sinning in the Hallway 39
Stupid 40
Summer Vacation 41
Summer 42
Taking Tests on Monday 43
Teachers. Issues. Tissues. 44
Teacher's Questions 45

The Ants in Tommy's Pants 46
The Backpack Backbox 47
The Death of a Classmate 48
The Dream Children 49
The Garden in My Classroom 50
The Hidden Stair 51
The Late School Bus 52
The Lunch Line Pioneer 53
The Mouse in School 54
The Shows of Sixth-Grade Girls 55
The Silent E Poem 56
The Teacher's Messy Desk 57
The Week Before Spring Break 58
Three Little Girls 59
Tweenitis 60
Autumn Leaves 61
Wearing Costumes to School 62
When Grandpa Was a Schoolboy 63
When the Schoolyard Melts in March 65

Recess Ain't Easy

At dinner each night I get questions.
"How was school?" and "What did you learn?"
"Can you show me what you have for homework?"
"At the drinking fountain, did you nicely wait your turn?"

Well, I've got important issues of my own,
But there seems to be no room for me to say,
"At school we've got us a recess problem
And it has to do with what we play!"

Teacher lets us take a ball outside
After everybody is finished with their lunch,
And all the students in my class gather round it
In a loud and shoving bunch.

Some think the ball is made to throw,
But some say it's just to kick,
And a couple favor basketball,
And several mention sticks.

In some games, you can't use your feet,
And in some games, that's all you use.
And some kids say we must wear special gloves,
And special hats and special shoes.

One kid says that football helmets
Put the icing on the cake,
But others say unless you've got a diamond,
You've gone and made a big mistake.

By then, the bell has sounded,
And it's time to go inside
And none of us played nothing,
And the ball is left outside.

Perhaps tomorrow we can figure out
A game we all decide we like to play.
See, I do have stuff we can discuss
When we talk about my day!

Recipe for Trouble

Eighteen boys in a classroom
Is "trouble served on toast."
Or, if you are a doctor,
It is "trouble…diagnosed!"

I pity the girls in the classroom.
They have to put up with the noise,
The confusion, the messing around,
Cooked up by these eighteen boys!

REMEMBERING!

Remembering stuff is funny,
because REMEMBERING is not all the same.
I often forget to do homework,
but I remember my friends' middle names.
I forget to remember to clean up my room; my coat I leave at school.
But I never forget the phone numbers of friends. THAT...I make a rule!

I wonder, what's up with the way my brain works?
I think it must like my friends!
But I think that my thinker's not working too well;
I hope it's not part of a trend!
Remind me to remind my brain to remember to think of the stuff that
my teachers want me to recall.
And if you don't remember to remind me, I doubt if I'll do it at all!

All the Stuff I Know

My grades can be misleading.
They don't reveal all I know
About what's real important.
So, let me show you so....

I know that peanut butter
Tastes really fine on cheese,
And milk squirts out your nose
If you're drinkin' when you sneeze.

I know that one of my shoelaces
Is most always left untied,
And that I'll never have clean gym clothes
No matter how I've tried.

I know my pencils all need sharpened,
And that erasers leave a smudge.
I know how to cut in lunch line,
And jammed lockers never budge.

I know I left my coat at school,
And now it's gone for good.
I know most desks are made of plastic,
Though they used to be of wood.

You'd think I'd almost get straight A's
With all that I could show,
But my teachers never check to see,
So, I'll guess we'll never know.

Assigned Reading

I've opened the textbook.
It's lookin' at me.
I'm lookin' right back,
But I can't seem to see.

It's not like my mother,
A TV, or game.
It's not got a plug-in.
It don't know my name.

I've covered it nicely
With a brown grocery sack.
It's real protected –
Still new, given back.

Time's passed, like a river,
But my brain just won't float.
The chapter's still quiet.
I can't read what's been wrote.

Teacher, please help me!
I'd like to get smart.
I'm trusting you know how
To get my book to start.

Braces

Kids' faces have braces
On all toothy places.
From crooked to straight, these braces replace.
From wiggly to steady, these braces displace.

Just in case
You've got some space,
I think you'd better get a brace.
This metal brace will the space erase.

Above your chin
Begins your grin.
If you're a youth, your grin has tin!
If you're a kid, your smile has style!

Bringing Elephants to School

My class is doing "Show 'n Tell",
And us kids like this a lot;
We get to bring amazing things
We've found, and own, and bought.

Next week's topic is "My Pet."
And we bring 'em to our grade
To show off to our classmates
In a big ol' pet parade!

Billy's got an ant farm,
And Sally's pet's a cat.
Freddy's got a puppy,
And Mike's got a nice white rat

Some kids will just bring pictures
Of the pet they dream about
And talk about their "photo pet",
But that's real boring...there's no doubt,

This project's got me thinking BIG...
Compared to Billy's ants.
So, I up and told my buddies
That I own an elephant!

Now I don't really own an elephant,
But that is what I said,
So now I've got to get one
Or my reputation's dead.

I've got to check out pet stores
And the circus and the zoo
To see if they would lend me
An elephant or two.

If I can pull this pet thing off
And bring an elephant with me,
They'll talk about MY "Show 'n Tell"
For years...I guarantee!

But just in case some accident
Pops up to mess my plan:
I'll just bring along a piece of rope
And pretend he got loose...and he ran!

"Bus Left"

"I've been bus left! I've been bus left!"
Rang the cry from down the hall.
"I've done been stranded at my school.
I don't understand the why at all!"

A look of sheer amazement was on her tear-streaked face.
Crumpled up beside her feet, her ragged book bag looked asleep.
One shoe's lace was trailing limply in her wake,
Her other shoe had lost its lace.

"I didn't even miss the bus. It went and just missed me.
For I had lots of errands after school I had to do
And each was more important than the last one.
Lots of stuff was all stacked up. And I had friends I had to see."

"I ran to turn a book in so I wouldn't get a fine,
Then I was got to feelin' thirsty, so I thought I'd get a Coke,
But I was out of money. Not a nickel. Not a penny. I was broke!
Fortunately, I recalled that on the playground I once lost a shiny dime!"

"I found that dime and three lost coats. I took the coats to Lost 'n
Found.
And that made me remember that my gym clothes needed washed,
So, I went to the locker room and stopped to shoot a couple hoops.
By then I knew it was getting' late. The bus would soon be around."

"So, after goin' to the bathroom and washing my hands real good,
I went and waited for the bus just like I knew I should.
'Cept nobody was waitin' with me. I thought they must be sick.
I'd gotten all my errands done, and I was feelin' pretty slick!"

"But then the principal started turning out the lights
And told me that 'less Mama came I'd most likely spend the night!
Man, oh man, I liked to choke! I ran to find a phone
To call my mom to come get me and cart me off to home!"

"Mama wasn't happy. She said I had "Bus-Left-i-tis."
And like as not would lose my head if it wasn't tied on tightest.
She said that I'd not only missed the bus, but TV for that night,
Even though I was not to blame…not even in the slightest!"

Cafeteria

My school's cafeteria is a most amazing place,
A cross 'tween Mama's kitchen and a scene from outer space.
For there's Randy in the corner, slurping soup from his plastic fork;
Ted and Sara, they're a'fussin...she just called Ted a "dork."
And Dixie wants ONLY French fries (seems she's low on fried in grease),
And the teachers in the back row are just lookin' for some peace.
There's about a thousand students, though they're hard to count in
flight,
And the noise is like a freight train fallin' off a cliff at night.
Oh, the lines are movin' slowly like molasses in the cold,
And by the time we see the food it's bound to be real old.
The milk will be expired, and the bread is turnin' green,
But the green beans will be browning...they're the worst I've ever seen!
The jello chews like rubber (though it's colored real nice),
And the cashier charged me plenty. I think she counted twice.
But even if it's noisy, and even if the lines are long,
I wouldn't miss a single day, 'cuz that's where I belong.
I get to see most all my friends and sit with Liz and Jane.
And, really, the food is pretty good; it's just the thing kids do...
COMPLAIN!

Capturing Kids' Hearts

To notice the reach of a child,
And lower yourself to their need,
Is one of life's most precious moments.
It's life's plan made real by deed.

To live so that lives of our children
Are richer by our having been
Brings power to the words of the Savior
And insight about what they mean.

So, capture young hearts in your travels.
Let living and service be one.
And know, with the faith of a child,
That life's best day hasn't yet come.

Caught in a Daydream

I just heard teacher ask a question,
Hooked to a name like mine,
But my mind was off a dreamin';
So, a good answer was hard to find.

I tried to pull an answer
From all the stuff I know:
"The capitol of Illinois?
I'd bet bucks on Chicago."

"Chicago?" asked my teacher,
In a tone of disbelief,
"This is science class, you slacker!"
Oh, I was headin' for some grief.

"So, what was the question?"
I was trying to reconnect.
"Volcanoes? Frogs? My project?
Have I stumbled on it yet?"

"The question I just asked you,
And that liked to shake your brain
Was, "What's the smallest planet?"
I held back a smart refrain....

Instead of searching blindly
For an answer in my mind
I devised a clever process
To get my thinkin' to unwind.

"Teacher, let's just try this out
And see if it will go:
Don't never ask me no question
'Less the answer's CHICAGO!"

Now, I'm sitting in the office
With demerits in my hand,
Just for tryin' to help my teacher
Ask me things I understand.

Cheerleaders

Some are fat, and some are thin.
Some are short, and some are tall.
But no matter how they differ,
Some things apply to ALL!

ALL cheerleaders have perfect hair
And makeup done just so.
I guess it's 'cuz they face the fans
And all their faces show.

Now, at the places you see cheering...
At them games they play at schools...
There must be special "cheerin' books"
Plumb full up with make-up rules.

I don't reckon that I've seen this book,
But I'm guessin' that it's there.
'Else, how could all them young ladies
Have that almost perfect hair?

They may never check the scoreboard
To see who's in the lead,
But just let a hair get out of place,
And you'll see a girl in need!

I really think cheerleaders
Are most often understood:
It's not their job to help us win;
Their job is lookin' good!

Crayons

I busted up my crayons
Colorin' maps and doin' art,
So, I keep the pieces in my pocket,
And I think that's pretty smart.

That way they're real handy
When I need 'em real quick.
I just peek into my pocket
And see which one I'll pick.

I use magenta for my homework,
And for science I use green.
But for spellin' I need yellow
So, my mistakes are hardly seen.

Black is for what I use in history...
All them men and wars and dates.
I also press down real hard
(It helps to keep things straight!)

Now, blue I save for numbers
'Cuz that is how I feel.
My math grade's always sorta low,
So, blue's perfect...it's ideal.

I write stories in all colors,
Savin' orange for nouns and such.
And brown I use for adverbs
'Cuz I don't understand 'em very much.

That's how I use my crayons
Now that they're short and broke.
Besides, I think it's sorta festive
To use crayons as a joke.

My teacher must not get the joke,
For he only shakes his head
And just accepts my papers.
Then he marks 'em up in RED!

"Don't Call on Me" List

Mama and Daddy don't like it…
Getting phone calls about dinnertime.
They tell all them "tele-phone-marketers"
that by callin' they're wastin' their dime!

I saw on the news just this morning
That there's a new, national "Don't Call Me" list
That Mama and Daddy can sign up for,
And I thought up a kid-friendly twist!

My teachers all call on us children
To answer the questions they've got
But often we don't know the answers,
So, our chance at a good grade gets shot.

I suggest that us kids start a program,
We'd call it the "Don't Call on Me."
And if we sign up, then teachers can't ask
Any questions. Our good grades would be guaranteed!

Dressing in Style

It's hard to dress in style
When you're livin' with your folks.
What I think's mighty stylish,
Mom and Daddy think's a joke.

I suggest I'd like an earring,
And they suggest back, "NO!"
I mentioned I liked saggy pants,
But they don't like my underwear to show.

I told them that a fishnet shirt
Would cool me as I ran,
But they said while I was running
I'd best come up with a plan.

"A plan?" I asked. "What do you mean?"
They clarified their intent:
If I started wearing just what I liked,
They'd begin to charge me rent.

Well, since I have no money.
No income, wealth, or job,
I guess I'll just keep wearing
Stuff that makes me look a slob.

My parents like the way I look,
As do the teachers at my school.
It's just the guy who sees me in my mirror
That thinks that I'm not cool.

Excuse ME!

"My dog ate my homework,"
Is so, SO 5th grade!
It's time that some better
Excuses were made!

Now, don't show your teachers
This poem full of pranks.
Just use them in YOUR school,
And then tell me, "Thanks!"

"My homework was written
On paper so light
That it got blown out my window
By a breeze in the night."

"You said we must use pencil,
And a pen was all I had
So, I decided not to do it
Just in case I'd make you mad."

"I'm sure I must have done it,
'Cuz I do just what you say,
So, I'm guessing that crooks swiped it
When I went outside to play!"

"I'm still hazy on the fine points,
But some little, greenish men
Said they liked to borrow homework
From us Earth kids now and then."

"Please check through the homework pile.
Are there some that are not signed?
If so, the one with all good answers
Is almost certain mine!"

"I tucked it in my textbook,
But then it got bizarre!
My textbook ATE my homework
Like it was a chocolate bar!"

Well, there're some new ideas
But they've got no guarantee.
So, if they don't work out with YOUR teacher,
Please don't say they came from me!

16

Figurative Language...NOT!

Mrs. Johnson told us students
That a poem we had to write
Chock full of things she's grading.
I tried real hard to get it right.

I wrote for a thousand hours
Trying to invent a hyperbole,
But when I finished writing,
No hyperbole did I see.

Next on Miss Tauna's wish list
Was to write a simile.
But I never seemed to write one.
My brain was like a busted knee!

Metaphor? I'd sooner find
My basketball was a spaceship.
So, no metaphor was in my poem.
It sure gave me the slip!

I couldn't even say
Per.. son..i..fi..ca..tion.
So, my poem just sat there blinking
Like an owl left in the sun.

Now Mrs. Johnson's waiting
For me to turn stuff in,
But I didn't do my homework,
So, I'll probably lose my skin!

Final Score: 35-0

My middle school has a football team,
And I am on the team.
They let me wear a uniform and helmet.
It's almost like a dream!

We practice hard right after school.
Our coach's name is "Coach".
(Although, when he's teaching science,
His name is Mr. Roche.)

A lot of us are sort of small,
And some can't run too fast.
And all of us have trouble
Catching balls that others pass.

We may be weak in speed and skill,
But we're strong in other ways.
We never try to hog the ball,
And we know almost all the plays.

We finally got to ride a bus
To play another school.
We did our homework on the ride—
Coach said it was a rule!

We rode and rode and rode the bus.
The driver looked at maps.
We stopped at lots of railroad signs,
And Coach took several naps.

We finally reached the other school
And we all ran to the field.
It made me think of knights of old,
Dressed in their armor with a shield.

I guess the other boys on the other team
Had also thought of knights,
For when they saw us in our suits,
They all cheered, "Fight! Fight! Fight!"

We hadn't thought to plan a cheer,
They took us by surprise.

Then Dusty Simmons shouted back,
"We're not even gonna cry!"

Coach must have thought of something new,
So, he turned and tried to speak.
Then he patted Dusty's helmet,
And his voice seemed liked a squeak.

"Men," he said, It's our first big game.
We stood up real tall.
"If we all play hard this afternoon,
I'll buy you burgers at the mall...."

We played real hard and were good sports.
We shared the ball a lot,
But after just four quarters
They said we had to stop.

We cheered and hollered, "Fight! Fight! Fight!"
When we got off at the mall.
And we wore our uniforms to dinner,
And we didn't feel small.

We felt like we were winners
As we rode back to our school,
And when Coach asked how we liked the game,
Dusty Simmons shouted, "COOL!"

I'm so proud I'm on our football team
And do you know what I like most?
I can't remember what the score was,
But I'll bet that it was close!

Friday

Weekends start at three o'clock
Most Fridays of the year,
And they end on Monday mornings
'Bout nine months of every year.

You see, I am a student
At middle school, down the street,
And they most expect to see me
Every morning in my seat.

And almost every mornin'
('Lessen I'm sick and like to die)
I show up with books and pencils
And I listen and I try.

But even though I work all week
To do what makes me smart,
I mostly like my Fridays
'Cuz they're my favorite part!

Of all the times and all the days,
My favorite comes at three
On each and every Friday…
'Cuz that's when THEY SET ME FREE!

Geography

My teacher said Geography is about where stuff is at.
Like towns and lakes and mountains and places that are flat.
Sometimes teacher spins the globe then stops it with a tap,
And then we children gather 'round and gaze upon the map.

Other times, she pulls down maps from a roll above the board,
And she points to things explorers found and places they explored.
And once I opened an Atlas on a shelf in the school library,
And I saw six maps of Africa and one of Tennessee.

I guess each place is on a map. It helps to keep things straight.
Things like countries, oceans, rivers, all directions, and my state.
It really gets confusing. There's too much – I wish she'd stop!
'Cuz all that I can remember is that North is at the top!

Gravity

In school I learned that apples
Fell on Isaac Newton's head
And made him discover gravity…
Leastwise, that's what my science teacher said.

I too discovered gravity,
And this is what I found
While skateboarding in the park…
The business end of gravity is right smack on the ground!

Guarantees for Kids

If kids came with papers
Like all used cars do,
We'd have us a way
To check kids that are new.

Are you ornery? Or silly?
We'd just look at your note.
Mean? Want to come here?
Your chance is remote.

Now, smart ones?
We want 'em
To come to our school.
Just don't send 'em dumb!

If each new kid came
With a strict guarantee,
If they didn't work out...
We'd send 'em back... FREE!

Hall Lockers

My locker's stuck! I can't get in!
My books are locked in tight,
So, I've been kickin' and a'bangin'
On the door to make it right.

If I just had me some dynamite,
Or a chain saw, or a drill,
I might break in to free my stuff.
Now, THAT would be a thrill!

My locker jams 'bout once a day.
It's like a trash compactor.
To take home all the junk inside
I'd need a trailer and a tractor.

I think I got the "locker answer",
And it wasn't very tough:
Just get us some bigger lockers,
Or kids with smaller stuff.

Halloween Dinner

I'm almost afraid to eat my dinner
When Halloween is here,
Because all the food in sight
Now causes me great fear.

Fried chicken? Not a chance!
Just the thought of all those BONES
Reminds me of spooky skeletons
And causes me to groan!

Jell-O? Like, not even!
Just mentioning that jiggly treat
Makes me think of goo and slime.
I turn white as a sheet!

Spaghetti? You must be joking!
All those white and wiggly squirms
Are just too close to real, scary
Bats, and bugs, and worms!

I think I'm about to lose some weight.
I'll probably just waste away!
I doubt I can eat a single thing
Except all the candy I collect on that spooky day!

Halloween

Halloween sits like an orange pumpkin
On the last post
Of October's fence.

Rustlings in the corn stalks
Delight my ears
With imagined fears.

Is it a skeleton rummaging for a bone?
A mournful ghost, sad that it's alone?
Perhaps a rat. Bare-tailed and fat?
Or a pitch-black vampire bat?

Or just October's quiet sigh,
Recalling memories
As it waves goodbye?

Homework

Working on homework and getting it done
Is not always easy and often not fun!
So, I sometimes don't do it. My paper's a mess.
"It fell in a puddle. My dog ate the rest!"

I whine when I get it, and my teacher looks stern.
She says homework helps me to get smart and learn.
Whenever my homework is not in on time,
The school phones to my house and heats up the line.

I stand next to teacher as she makes the call.
I know I'm in trouble, and tears start to fall.
"Dry it up, Buster!" My teacher's not glad.
And when she tells Mama, Mama gets mad!

Mama mad at teacher? That's a pig that's got one wing.
I should have done my homework to prevent this tragic scene.
I know that the best road for me to go down
Has me doing my homework as soon as it's found.

Do homework early. Do my best. Make sure all work is mine.
Be sure the numbers all add up. Never sloppy copy.
And get it in on time!

"I almost remember…"

I almost remember the answer.
It's right on the tip of my mind.
It's hiding someplace in my memory,
But it sure is elusive to find.

I knew that this test would be tricky.
I knew that I should study hard,
But I chose to go play with my buddies,
Shooting hoops in Jimmy's back yard.

I did put my notes in my backpack.
I carried them onto the bus.
But when I threw my backpack at Russell,
My notes got tore up in the fuss.

My textbook? It's still in my locker,
Or maybe I lost it last week.
It's hard to keep track of my studies,
I've got a forgetful technique!

I'd like to do good on my schoolwork.
I think about getting good grades.
But whenever I plan to remember,
My rememberin' just sorta fades!

All's I'm doin' is slouching and scowlin',
With a blank look all over my face.
I haven't even written an answer…
I've got nothing to even erase!

I'd like to pretend that I'm dreaming.
Or that maybe I'm under a spell,
And "POOF!" like a puffball in August
I'll remember and really do quite well.

If Sixth Grade Ran the World

If Sixth Grade ran the world,
It wouldn't be like now.
There'd be a whole lot less of walking slow
And a whole lot more of WOW!

There'd be ice cream for breakfast,
And there'd be some more for lunch.
Mushy food could not be served,
And snack time would follow brunch.

Homework would be movies,
With amusement parks for tests.
We'd play all day with all our friends
And pass silly notes to pests.

We never would pick up our rooms.
The floor could not be found!
And we'd pass out books to teachers...
You know, the other way around!

We'd wear our hair all whichy way,
And sometimes sleep 'till noon.
We'd slurp our milk and Jell-O
And eat peas with plastic spoons.

We'd giggle when we heard a burp
And laugh loud at every joke.
We'd spend our money on useless stuff
And buy some more stuff if it broke.

If Sixth Grade ran the world,
A lot of stuff would switch.
We'd all throw sticks at recess,
And we'd scratch at every itch.

Oh, if Sixth Grade ran the world...!

Inside Recess

We can't go out for recess!
It's raining cats and dogs.
Teacher says it's too wet for playing,
Unless you're a fishy or a frog.

I close my eyes and wonder
If I had scales instead of skin,
And flippers 'stead of fingers,
Would Teacher keep me in?

Lipstick

Lipstick's quite an issue
When I'm getting dressed for school.
Mama says I'm much too young,
But I think lipstick's cool.

So, Mama and I worked it out
And with this issue came to grips:
I DO get to wear my lipstick...
But only on my bottom lip!

Locker Clean-Out

Teacher says our lockers
Must be cleaned before we go.
I guess she hasn't peeked inside
My locker, or she'd know.

She'd know it's packed with memories
Which are special just to me,
But they're designed to look like garbage
So, they're difficult to see.

There are the notes that Betty wrote me
(I'm the one that she adores!),
And first semester's gym socks
Are growing on its floor.

There are tests that I did well on,
And some homework that was "lost."
There's even one green sandwich
That I really oughta toss!

My locker is a kid museum,
A trove of useful stuff.
It's just sorta short on neatness,
But all year 'twas good enough.

Now, teacher says to clean it…
To toss what's stuffed inside.
I'd kind of like to seal it,
But with teacher's orders I'll abide.

"Goodbye, Ol' This Year's Locker,
You've been a friend to me.
A place to store my precious trash,
But now I'll set ya free!"

Lost 'n Found

Mama called the school today
And said she's coming quick
To take me to the doctor
To see if I was sick.

I don't feel sick nor puny,
But I'm waitin' by the door.
And I've started getting wiggly
'Cuz sittin' quiet's quite a chore.

I dropped my books a while back.
It sounded like a shot,
And it must of spooked the secretary
'Cuz she jumped a real lot.

Then I dropped my lunch box,
And the thing just come unglued.
And when my apple rolled across the floor,
The secretary squished it with her shoe.

Then I knocked my trombone over,
And it liked to wake the dead.
I peeked over at Ms. Secretary,
And she's just shakin' off her head!

I hope my Mama hurries up
To take me to the doc,
For Ms. Secretary's getting' restless,
And she's lookin' at the clock.

I just heard the secretary say
She'll soon be lockin' down,
And if my Mama isn't punctual
She'll put me in lost 'n found!

Math Grade

I got my grade in math today.
It like to knocked me flat!
Teacher said I'd made an F.
I think we need to chat.

I told her I could really add
And showed her what I meant
By countin' up the nights I'd spent
In my backyard in my tent.

I told her I'd counted tile rows
On the floor and overhead
And then I up and multiplied...
I done it in my head.

I'd looked out of the window
At the flag up in the sky
And by lookin' at the shadow
I know the flagpole's real high.

When Randy brought his birthday cake
For all us kids to share,
It was me who knew how to divide it
So, all the slices were cut fair.

And I know teacher says a hundred
Is the best grade that I can get,
But when I subtract all of my zeros...
I'm a long way from it yet.

But me and teacher chatted
And I think we've compromised
With me promising to do better,
To pay more attention...and to apologize!

Retention

My teacher kept me after class
And gave me quite a fear.
She said if I did not improve
I'd be retained again next year!

I'm guessing that my teacher
Has also been retained.
She's been teaching kids for years,
But in sixth grade she's remained.

The South Carolina Sleigh Ride

Christmas time reminds me
Of trees with pretty lights.
Of snowflakes in the frosty air.
And sleigh rides late at night.

I think a lot of jingle bells
And horses pulling sleighs,
But where I live there's not much snow...
Instead, we've got hard red clay!

So now I dream of tiny wheels
On that sleigh to make it go.
Otherwise, out where I live
Our sleighs would pull SOOOO slow!

School Bus

The yellow bus holds children,
And I ride it every day.
In morning, it heads to my school.
And at night we go the other way.

I feel so gosh durned special
In my seat upon the bus
'Cuz when we flash the blinking lights
All traffic stops for us.

Our driver is so careful
As she makes our daily drive.
I'll bet she gets most every child
Home safely and alive!

In the morning when I get on,
The bus is sleepy quiet,
But after school as we head home
It's like a prison riot!

After lots of careful study
I think I've finally figured out
What drivin' yellow buses
Is really all about.

I now know just why my driver
Takes me home the shortest way
And even makes suggestions
That will help us with our day.

Such things as, "Y'all be quiet
So, you don't wake up the dead!"
Now, that is shore 'nuff helpful,
So, I sit silent next to Fred.

Sometimes it's, "Close your eyes now
And just listen to the sound
Of all your little bitty brains
A'sloshing all around."

Perhaps it's, "In your pockets
Is the place to keep your hands!"
I guess that's so we don't borrow
Some OTHER child's hands!

Mostly, it's, "Quit yer fussing
And lock the winders tight."
I guess this keeps out pirates
Who are itchin' for a fight.

But the most useful of her hollers
Comes on Fridays of each week...
When she yells, "I'm 'bout to unload y'all
At the next stop in a heap!"

I think that's some useful information
For me to plan THAT stop,
And I'll plan to be last off
So, I'll end up on the top!

Sitting in The Hallway

I'm sitting in the hallway,
And the classroom door is closed.
The teacher told me to sit out here...
Now, why do you suppose?

The story that I'm telling
To my Mom and Dad tonight
Is that she's scolding all my classmates
And didn't want ME to see the fight.

The more I think it over,
The clearer that it gets:
I'm not in trouble out here,
For I'm my teacher's pet!

She likes me more than the others,
And she wants to spare me pain
From listenin' to her holler
At Will, and Kris, and Jane.

I really should thank my teacher
For treatin' me so fine
And tryin' to spare my feelings
When the rest are out of line!

Stupid

Stupid's got no limits.
Its expanse cannot be found.
Like picnic ants, it can't be detoured.
It's like the sniffer of a hound.

There ain't no shot for stupid.
It just shows up like the sun.
So, no cure can come from doctors,
And its course must just be run.

But like the sore throats
That I had when I was young,
Stupid can be diagnosed
When a fool sticks out his tongue!

Prevention is the answer.
So, when stupid first appears,
Shut your eyes so you can't see it
And stick your fingers in your ears!

Summer Vacation

The day I've waited months is here...
School is finally out!
No tests or grades for ninety days.
I let out a mighty shout,

"No need for books or pencils!
My homework's REALLY lost!
All projects to the trashcan!
My backpack must be tossed!"

The final bell! I race for home
To play in my back yard,
But skid into a sudden stop...
The truth just hit me hard!

I'm thirty minutes into summer.
The school year's finally through,
But I'm already feeling bored.
No school? What's there to do?

Summer

Like a puppy,
Summer pokes its green nose
Into my classroom,
Begging me outside
To play.

It doesn't understand
That there are still
Two weeks of school.

Sit, Summer!
Stay!

Taking Tests on Mondays

Taking tests on Mondays
Ought to be against the law
Because it forces me to try to think
Before my brain can thaw.

My brain is like a block of ice
And school is like the sun
So, it's almost always Wednesday
Before my thoughts can run.

Tuesday's just like Monday,
No need to mention more.
And on Thursday, when it gets in gear,
My brain's already sore.

Now, on Friday I am ready.
My brain is running great...
As long as tests aren't early,
Or too hard, or long, or late.

Really, I guess the best day
To see what all I know
Is Saturday, but there's no school...
Oh well, that's how it goes!

Teachers. Issues. Tissues

I've got a rubber band knotted up in my hair!
When I sat down, there was gum on my chair!
I need the blue pencil, but Leonard won't share!
Why can't we just sit on the floor over there?

My flip-flop's toe grabber just came undone!
I'm walking this fast 'cuz you said not to run.
I don't think that fractions and decimals are fun!
If I finish my test first, does it mean that I've won?

I can't zip my zipper! It's grabbed on my shirt!
I spilled the ant farm all over my skirt!
Isn't it cool how dried mud turns to dirt!
In the lunchroom today, can we first eat dessert?

Look! Both my sneakers just came untied.
Instead of a line, can't we walk side by side?
Why does your teacher's chair need to be wide?
Julie said I look silly so that's why I cried!

When will we learn that big deals in big places
Can be resolved with hugs and tied-up shoelaces?
If teachers were in charge of the world's big issues
They'd answer our questions…and then pass out some tissues!

Teacher's Questions

I really like my teacher,
And I think she likes me too.
She smiles when she sees me,
And sometimes she hugs me, too.

But I've started thinkin' lately
That she's really not that bright
'Cuz she keeps on askin' questions...
With answers even I get right!

Seems she's not sure who is President;
She wants to know, "What is a noun?"
And when she asks, "Who's done their homework?"
She asks it with a frown.

She keeps askin' who's the scoundrel
Who kicked the football on the roof?
And she keeps bugging me about my math
And askin' for my proof.

I know that teacher's getting' older,
Since she's taught since the year of one,
But I hope I've answered all her questions,
And I hope that she is done.

If she's gotten all the answers
To all the questions that she had
I know in some small way I've helped her.
And I smile...and I'm glad!

The Ants in Tommy's Pants

"Tommy, quit your wigglin'!
Just sit quiet at your desk.
Your classmates all need think time
As they try to pass this test."

The teacher's look was get-to-work.
Her words backed up her stare.
But Tommy just kept wiggling 'round,
Almost fallin' from his chair.

"Thomas, it's the last time!
I've done gone and told you twice.
If you continue with your fussin'
I'm gonna quit with bein' nice...."

"Ms. Brooks," said little Tommy,
As he fiddled with his pants,
"I'm thinkin' I found the problem,
And that problem is there's ANTS!"

Ms. Brooks got Tommy standin',
And she brushed him up and down.
Shore 'nuff, she found a bunch of ants.
They was crawlin' all around!

As we tried to solve the mystery,
Ms. Brooks got herself a hunch.
Seems Tommy filled his pockets
With some pizza scraps at lunch.

In his haste to hit the playground,
He didn't want to stand in line
To place his garbage in the trashcan,
So that's why them ants came in to dine!

I guess we passed the math test,
But who knows what were our scores?
For what us kids will all remember
Is them ants in Tommy's drawers!

The Backpack Backbox

I got me a brand-new backpack
To start my sixth-grade year.
It had lots of little pockets.
It was lovely. It was dear.

But in a week, it lost a buckle,
And the zipper stuck one day,
So, from then on, I could only
Cram my notebooks in halfway.

It ripped out real drastic
On a cold November day,
And from then on it dropped pencils.
(I lost five most every day!)

I told my Mom about my troubles,
And I begged her for some cash
To buy me another backpack,
But my dreams got broke and smashed.

She said that I'd been careless,
And I'd caused her grief and pain...
Like when I left my tattered backpack
In the back yard in the rain.

Now, I don't have ANY backpack,
'Cuz it ended in the trash.
And I can't get me another
'Cuz Mom won't cough up any cash.

I'm just gonna BUILD a backpack...
It just sorta dawned on me...
Out of the sturdy cardboard box
That once housed our new TV!

The Death of a Classmate

No books will ever open
From the student's hands again.
And her locker's combination
Will never need to spin.

Her backpack is still hanging
On the hook beside the door.
No need to check for childish notes
That may have fallen on the floor.

I close my eyes and she still sits
Across from all her friends.
And I hear her voice at recess
In the breathing of the wind.

As she enters school in Heaven
With new friends on every side,
I know she'll always get straight A's...
My classmate who has died.

The Dream Children

The dream children in the corners,
In the shadows, on the precipice,
Need teachers who can hear songs without sound.
See art without color.
Tell stories without endings.
Teachers who can reach across chasms
Without bridges.

The dream children need dream teachers
Who inspire one more reach into the air
With trust they'll find a teacher there.

The Garden in My Classroom

My classroom is my garden,
And my students are the seeds.
In late summer I open envelopes,
And I shake out all their needs.

All fall I labor long
To tend each needful row
And nurture every tender shoot
With all the love I can bestow.

In winter, under icy blasts,
It's hard to see beneath the snow
And still insure my efforts
Are helping flowers grow.

Yet, each spring I see my garden
As tiny flowers begin to show,
And I realize that lives are richer
Because of the love that I can sow.

The Hidden Stair

If you stand at the base of a big ol' hill
And count every rock—as some folks will—
You can imagine the peak's plumb out of your reach,
So, you can't ever learn what a mountain can teach.

But if, instead of the rocks of strife,
You see steppingstones on the path of life,
Each placed with a master mason's care,
What you have found is the hidden stair.

Each mountain that lies in life's thoroughfare
Is both a curse and an answered prayer.
For some, each mountain is just silent rock;
It takes a dreamer to hear a mountain talk.

The Late School Bus

When the bell sounds at the end of day,
Students rush out the door
And exit from the building.
Until tomorrow, they're no more.

But...some children just don't leave the school.
They hang around and fuss.
It's not that they don't have a home;
They're just waiting for the bus!

The bus schedules do confuse me,
With their precious student freight.
In the morning they bring kids early,
But after school they take 'em late!

The Lunch Line Pioneer
(Sung to the tune of The Yellow Rose of Texas)

In history class last Friday
I learned of pioneers
Who drove their covered wagons
Way out West for years and years.

Today the lunch line isn't moving,
And I'm starving as I stand.
And I'm thinkin' of them pioneers
And how they crossed our land.

I recall the Donner's party
Getting' plumb stuck in the snow,
So, they started eatin' people
Just to make their hunger slow.

Although I am near starvin',
It doesn't make much sense
For me to gnaw my classmates,
And my reason is immense!

See, I need my friends at recess
To play football in the yard.
And if I up and ate 'em,
Playin' catch would be too hard.

The Mouse in School

"Vermin! Vermin!" our teacher's voice was shrill!
And that much exuberance gave us school kids a thrill.
Now, our school is not noted for frequent excitement,
So, we take what we get and create us an event.

Teacher scrambled on top her desk. My, but she could scoot!
And Johnny started throwing spitballs as fast as he could shoot.
Betty grabbed the dustpan, and Larry poked the broom
Behind the dusty bookcase and caused that mouse to zoom!

Kids were tipping over desks and books were in the air.
You'd of thought only a grizzly bear could cause so great a scare.
Finally, though, the game wore down. The mouse tore out the door.
And teacher crawled down off her desk and stood upon the floor.

"Now, Children, like I was saying before I climbed to get a view,
Find your notes, dust off your books; it's time for a review.
Who can tell me, Children, if your brains have got calmed down,
Is "vermin" ...like I used it...an adjective or noun?"

The Shoes of Sixth-Grade Girls

They wear their shoes…like normal folks…
Upon their feet; one right, one left.
But there the "normal" ends, it seems,
For sixth-grade girls have big shoe dreams!

Instead of buying books to read,
Or putting money in the bank,
Sixth grade girls come up with schemes,
For sixth-grade girls have big shoe dreams!

On Saturday they stalk the malls
With money pestered from their folks.
In their eyes the shoes stores gleam,
For sixth-grade girls have big shoe dreams!

They tote shoes home…sack after sack.
Then toss them on their bedroom floor.
They like to see them all, it seems,
For sixth-grade girls have big shoe dreams!

The Silent E Poem

I'm pretty poor at spelling,
So, I think it's sorta funny
If words aren't hard enough to spell,
Someone adds a "Silent E."

For example, there's a shoe store,
In a town just down from me,
That's called the "Olde Shoe Shoppe."
Not only did they add two "Silent E's"…they found a "Silent P"!

It's got me very puzzled,
But since my spelling grade is low
I need me some extra credit.
I wrote a note and told my teacher so.

"Misse Smithe, I ame the studente
Whoe hase learnede of silente e.
Coulde youe please give me extra pointse
Fore everye one youe seeeeee?"

The Teacher's Messy Desk

My teacher's desk is piled high
With papers, books, and stuff.
And if it ever avalanched,
It'd kill a kid. Shore 'nuff!

That's why I never like
To stand by that dangerous mound
'Cuz if it ever hit a kid,
That kid would not be found!

Word has it that a while back…
I'm not sure of the date…
A kid went in for extra help.
The teacher was stayin' late.

Well, all was goin' peachy,
And the kid was getting' help,
But the mountain started movin',
And the kid let out a yelp.

Turned out it was his FINAL yelp.
No other sound he made
As all those books and paper
Covered him up like a grave.

They say his Momma came to school
To see if his body had been found,
But not even with a putty knife
Could he be scraped off the ground.

So, here's a word of good advice:
If y'all don't want to be mashed like that,
Don't never ask for extra help
Unless the teacher's desk is flat!

The Week Before Spring Break

I've got a great big problem,
And it has to do with time:
My school's clocks must be broken.
I'm about to lose my mind!

It's the week before vacation,
And I'm standing at the board
Writing out 100 times in chalk
"I'll not tell teacher I am bored."

But I AM bored, and I'm tired,
And I'm ready for a break.
So, I'm pretending like I'm sorry,
But I'm feeling like a fake.

I peek out of the window.
I see green grass and the sun.
I want so bad to be outside;
To fly a kite and run.

To Einstein, time was relative.
And E was MC squared,
But he's never come to my school,
So, I think he doesn't care.

Time is not MY relative!
I'm not concerned with E !
I sure hope they start vacation soon
So, I can just be free!

I'm ready for vacation,
And I know that teacher is
'Cuz she's writing on her notepad
"I MUST not kill these kids!"

I've written mine 'most thirty times,
But teacher's got me beat.
She's written hers a hundred times
EACH DAY FOR THE PAST WEEK!

Three Little Girls

Three little girls,
Sitting in a row.
One pitched a fit,
So, she had to go!

Two little girls,
Sitting in a row.
One kicked a rock
And stubbed her toe!

One little girl,
Sitting all alone.
Along came her bus,
So, she went home!

No little girls
Sitting in a row
When will they return?
I just don't know....

Tweenitis

I'm a student at a middle school,
And I'm feeling in between
So, I'm goin' to see my school nurse
To find out what it means.

I'm between K-5 and high school.
I'm between with most my likes;
I'm not ready to drive Daddy's car,
But I'm getting bored with riding bikes.

I'm making more decisions
'Bout my schooling and my life,
But I'm not always makin' good ones
So, it causes "Tweener's Strife."

The symptoms can be many,
But the common kinds are these:
Pouting, but soon shouting.
Teasing siblings. Climbing trees.

I've got a smarty answer
For each question that I'm asked.
I like to think I'm all grown up...
My childhood has passed.

I still like hugs from all my teachers
(Tho' I pretend I don't),
And when my teachers say to study
'Bout half the time I won't.

Don't ask ME to figure out
These symptoms and a cure;
That job is for my school nurse.
She'll fix me up, I'm sure!

Nurse says I've got TWEENITIS,
And no cure is yet in sight,
So, I'm still stuck in the middle...
Feelin' weird, but it's all right.

I'm getting used to my TWEENITIS.
Getting used to my disease.
In fact, I kind of like it.
So, just call me TWEENER, if you please!

Autumn Leaves

The rumpled autumn leaves,
From the maple, sycamore, and oak
Make me think that tiny forest folk
Must be a lot like me.

Leaping from their snuggly nests each morning,
Tossing aside their leafy covers
In their hurry to discover,
And leaving unmade beds behind—like me.

Wearing Costumes to School

I'd like to wear my costume…
For Halloween…to school.
But my teacher says to leave it home.
She said it is the rule!

I checked with all my classmates,
And they said she told 'em, too,
To leave their scary clothes at home
And keep 'em out of view.

I guess my teacher is a scardy cat
Who'd likely up and faint
If she saw me and my classmates
All dressed up in sheets and paint.

When Grandpa Was a Schoolboy

School was uphill from his house,
And his house uphill from school.
He always walked knee deep in snow.
I guess that was a rule.

He said they learned about three R's.
Today, I think we've just got one.
He said he remembers see-saws,
But my playground ain't got none.

Grandpa said that all their whiteboards
Ran on chalk and just were black.
When I asked about their backpacks,
He said back then they just used sacks!

He said they had things called filmstrips.
They was movies cut in bits.
But he said they didn't watch 'em often.
I guess their movies were not hits!

Their desks were big and heavy,
With a hole that held their ink.
I'm not too sure what they done with it,
But I think it was a drink.

A Big Chief made all their paper,
And their yellow pencils too.
They only had six crayons,
And they used paste instead of glue!

I listened close to what he said
As I sat on Grandpa's knee.
It's fun to learn about the time
When he was small like me.

When the Schoolyard Melts in March

When the glaciers on the playground
Recede like Siberia's polar ice,
A lot of things begin to show,
And most aren't very nice.

Is that a mammoth's floppy trunk
Sniffing from beneath the snow?
No, it's just Betty's dirty gym sock
She lost about three months ago.

Wow, looks like a wooly rhino
Thawing from its Arctic freezer!
Naw, just a teacher's fuzzy mitten
Lost by one of them ol' geezers.

A herd of little furry ponies...
A Scientific Channel TV deal...
Turn into plastic movie robots
Dropped from a happy meal.

Tusks become lost pencils,
And teeth but the doughy crusts
From Jimmy William's sandwich
He dropped while climbing on the bus.

It's fun to think that schoolyards
Conceal exciting things to find,
But the Viking's golden treasure
Turns out to be dried orange's rind.

I guess I'm almost ready
For the snow to melt away,
So, I won't have to worry
About the tricks my mind will play.

Growing up "poor and on horseback" as part of a ranching family on the Pine Ridge Reservation in South Dakota (Lakota Sioux) provided Ivan with opportunities and perspectives rare in today's world. As one of a class of three students in a one-room rural school, Ivan learned early the excitement of literacy and written words and their ability to enrich and narrate his world. Uniquely, Ivan was a minority in a Native culture not far removed from its roots on the open plains. His family's hired man, Paul Bear Saves Life, had been a baby at the massacre at Wounded Knee and Ivan's best friend was Chucky Looking Elk. Ivan has never forgotten these foundational life lessons on the high plains of the American West.

Ivan is certified as a public school superintendent, elementary principal, secondary principal, elementary supervisor, and secondary supervisor. He and his wife, Lynn, make their home in the foothills of the Blue Ridge Mountains in South Carolina. They have three children and four grandchildren.

www.ingramcontent.com/pod-product-compliance
Lightning Source LLC
Chambersburg PA
CBHW011218120626
46545CB00008B/3044